Technical Analysis In Day Trading

Day Trading Strategies to become a
Profitable Investor and How To Build a
Passive Income At Home

By
Lukas Bagopym

Table Of Contents

Technical Analysis In Trading

Trading v / s Investing

Another big difference between the two types of analysis is the goal. The technical analysis is based on short-term empirical data and is mainly used in trade. The fundamental analysis aims to support the investment department on a much larger and long-term scale. A trader's goal is to buy an asset so that it can be resold later at a higher price to benefit from the difference. This is a short-term process. On the other hand, an investor looks for assets that he believes will grow in value over time and makes purchases based on this premise, being aware that this process can take a long time and long term It may be difficult to understand what the difference between trading and investing is (the line between the two is fairly thin), but this is one of the main aspects that distinguish between fundamental and technical analysis.

After you better understand the difference between these two types of analysis, we will focus more on introducing technical analysis in the following sections.

Technical analysis methods

There are many methods used by technical analysis. However, they are divided into several specific classes:

1. Levels and lines of resistance and support
2. Technical indicators
3. Patterns on large parts of the diagram
4. Candle analysis
5. Trading volume

As a rule, experienced traders combine different techniques in their methods and wait for their mutual reaction. This response can be considered the most reliable to do business in the market.

Levels and lines of resistance and support

The price is constantly changing, this is what makes up a chart. There are peaks and dips that mark the highs and lows. If you draw a line along a series of highs or lows, this is known as a resistance or support line.

These are the values of the quotation marks where the cryptocurrency exchange rate is a significant obstacle after which reversal is possible. Horizontal support and resistance lines are called planes.

There is strong support in places where a large number of large purchase orders accumulate. The same applies to the level of resistance, which is determined by the existence of a significant list of sales orders. One of the main definitions for traders is the trend and the trend price movement. A trend is a channel that consists of parallel resistance and support lines.

The direction of the trend movement is determined by the slope of the lines. If they are up, the trend is said to be up. This means that cryptocurrency trading is done with a predominant number of purchases. The reverse is true for a downward trend. A side trend (or flat) is a movement where the resistance and support lines are horizontal and there is an approximate equality of sales and purchases.

Main characters of technical analysis

The figure is a picture that describes the price change of a crypto instrument that traders keep noticing on the chart.

Head and shoulders

The head and shoulders reversal pattern is quite common following a strong and long-lasting trend. The figure consists of three successive tips, the middle (head) of which is the highest and the other two tips on the sides (shoulders) are lower and almost the same.

1. Determination of the trend

First of all, there is an upward trend. This graphical model must be preceded by a strong upward trend.

2. Left "shoulder"

Then we wait for the formation of the left "shoulder", which looks like a new maximum on the map with the subsequent correction. In addition, the lowest correction point is usually not below the current trend line.

3. "head"

Now that the correction has been completed, it is the turn of the "head". It looks like strong price momentum in the direction of the current trend. It sets a new maximum, but the price immediately rolls back to the level from which the momentum started and breaks the current trend line. This raises doubts about the strength of the bull trend.

4. Right "shoulder"

However, the strength of the bulls is still enough to correct the situation. They enter the market and drive up the price. However, the lack of potential buyers means that the price cannot set a new maximum and rolls back and forms the right shoulder of the model. Although the theory assumes that the right and left "shoulders" are symmetrical, this is not always the case in practice.

5. Breakthrough of the neck line

After the price has dropped and no new maximum has been reached, it approaches the so-called "neck" line, which is held at the minima of the left "shoulder" and "head". The "neck" can have an upward slope , a horizontal position or a downward slope - depending on the correlation of the forces of bulls and bears. A classic sell signal appears when the price breaks the neckline.

6. Target win

It is recommended to exit this trading position after the price has covered a distance equal to the distance from the maximum of the "head" to the height of the "neck". However, this is just an approximate goal that needs to be refined with other tools such as support and resistance lines.

Raised floor or double lid

Double bottom is one of the most common patterns after a downward trend, double double after an upward trend. The figure "Double Bottom" is very similar to the figure "Double Top". They are identical, with the only difference that they reflect each other.

Usually, the classic raised floor suggests at least a small change in the direction of the trend. The main price movement, which is the double bottom, is considered the intersection of the resistance line from bottom to top.

Rectangular figure

The shape "rectangle" is easy to see in the table. The rectangle is a kind of pause in the trend, in which buyers and sellers are approximately the same. The peculiarities of the rectangle - smooth support and resistance lines; Support and resistance are the two horizontal sides of an imaginary rectangle.

The rectangle is a simple figure in technical analysis that shows the struggle between sellers and buyers.

Flag and pennant

The flag and pennant reflect a short consolidation phase as part of a dynamically developing price movement trend. Such models should be preceded by a major price change. The consolidation number itself is limited by parallel or slightly converging support and resistance lines, which form a flag-like figure, which is usually inclined or arranged horizontally against the direction of the trend. After the collapse, the price movement should repeat at least the distance covered before the figure was formed.

The market reduces everything

It is generally accepted that technical analysis is based on three basic principles or principles. The first is that the market action reflects everything you need to know about the price. This is extremely important because technical analysis underpins the concept that just by looking at market actions, we can get a good idea of future movements.

There are many things that can affect the price. This includes basic factors such as selling products and making a profit. political or business factors such as legislation, the appointment of a new CEO or changes in work practices; and psychological factors, such as whether the latest toy becomes a teenage fad or whether the Blackberry becomes a must for business reasons. By thwarting this and explaining that all of these factors, which may or may not be identifiable, are included in the price through market measures, the analyst can only focus on the market and does not require a group of research assistants.

If it seems that this is simplifying the situation too much, remember that all it really means is that supply and demand are demonstrated in market actions. Classical economics teaches us that supply and demand determine price - if demand exceeds supply, price will increase over time, also known as the bullish market. On the other hand, oversupply and low demand will inevitably lead to a falling price or a downward movement. What leads to the supply increasing or decreasing need not concern the technical analyst. the same with demand. The result is all that matters.

If you think about it, it makes our job a lot easier. If we can rely on just looking at price and volume (and we can) to get information about the impact of all these different influences, we will reduce the overall problem that we may have had to a manageable size. In fact, it's pretty neat how it works, since many of these factors that affect price are likely to be difficult to quantify.

By looking at what market action says about a stock or security price, we are letting the market tell which direction it will go, rather than trying to rethink buyers and sellers. There are certainly reasons for prices to rise and fall, but it is simply not necessary to know these reasons when predicting future movements.

It is an important principle of trading that you let the market tell you where you are going. Some people seem to think that they can control the market, or at least tell them where to go based on all sorts of sensible ideas. If you prepare to fight the market this way, you will end up losing because the market is bigger than every single participant. You have to learn to anticipate the river and walk with it.

The market shows trends

The second principle of technical analysis is that prices tend to move in trends. By this we mean that the rising price is likely to continue to rise; if it falls, it will continue to fall; and if it hovers at about the same level, it will continue to do what is sometimes referred to as moving sideways. Of course, none of these things go on forever, but it is generally expected that a trend will continue for a while before it changes. Many trading plans are based on this premise - you may have heard the phrase "let the trend be your friend", which means you should act to follow the existing trend. If you do something else, you are at higher risk.

We'll start with charting and the different chart types in the next module, but just to illustrate a "trend", here's a simple chart. You may be familiar with charts after you've considered trading. If not, you need to understand that they are one of the core tools available to the dealer. You have to learn everything you can about them.

Most charts that you use have the same basic layout. Time is along the horizontal or X axis and price is along the vertical or Y axis. Time can display minutes or hours during the day or days, weeks or months. As a rule, diagrams are displayed whose time scale is given in days. It is common to include only working days five days a week.

This graph alwaysshows an upward trend, with the price increasing over time. Note that it does not usually go straight up, but in a series of batches, with so-called "retracements" in between. Overall, this graph shows a very clear upward trend. Sometimes it is helpful to look at different time scales so you can see which direction the trend is going - for example, if you looked at a chart of the same stock as shown above, but with a different time scale that only showed you a retracement. You might think the stock was in a downtrend.

Advanced technical analysis: 5 key analysis techniques

Technical analysis is a form of analysis used by traders to evaluate future price promotions based on historical price data.

Many traders use technical indicators and chart analysis as an approach to analyze the markets and identify potential trading opportunities and suitable entry and exit points. This article looks at five advanced technical analysis approaches you can use to improve your trading strategy.

Many traders use candlestick charts when looking at price data, and it's easy to see why. Candlesticks present the battle between buyers and sellers in a very easy to interpret graphic way. Candlestick charts also have their own patterns, with many focusing on the psychology of the market and the constant struggle between buyers and sellers.

Bullish engulfing pattern

The bullish engulfing pattern occurs when a market is in a downtrend. Bullish engulfing patterns usually consist of two full candlesticks that span two periods (for example, an hour or a day). The first is a "down" or bearish candlestick, followed by an "up" or bullish candlestick covering the following period.

The size of the first candle can vary from chart to chart. The first candle usually means the end of falling market prices. The second candle in the pattern should be larger than the previous candle and cover (or gobble) the 'body' of the previous candle . The larger the second candle and the higher it advances, the stronger the signal.

Here is an example of the FTSE 100 index based on daily candles.

In this example, the market has been in decline for more than a week, but there is a relatively large upward day that completely overshadows the previous day's candle. Together, these two candles form the bullish engulfing pattern, indicating that the weakness is coming to an end and the trend may be reversing.

Bearish engulfing pattern

Bearish engulfing patterns are a reflection of the bullish variety, with the difference that the bearish engulfing pattern market goes higher, but then there is a candle in the opposite direction to the trend that devours the previous candle - which is a change in means mood from buying pressure to selling pressure.

As with the previous candlestick chart pattern, the first candle in this formation means that the current trend is coming to an end. The size of the first candle can vary from chart to chart, and it is the second or "devouring" candle that signals the trend change. In order to qualify as a bearish engulfing pattern, the second candle must completely devour the previous candle. Ideally, the high should be above the high of the previous candle and a new low should be created - which means renewed selling pressure downwards.

The following example shows the oil price and each candle represents one hour of trading.

As with all other trading strategies, candlestick charts should be used in conjunction with other forms of analysis to consider when market sentiment may change.

Bullish divergence signal

Many traders will use technical indicators to figure out market direction. You may have seen charts with stochastic oscillators, moving average convergence divergence (MACD) and other lines underneath the price. One variation of the indicator approach is to look for divergences. This is where the price does one thing but the indicator does something else - it can be a sign that a trend is running out of steam, offering the opportunity to profit from a move in the other direction. In the chart below, the price of gold has a relative strength index (RSI) shown below the price, which is always a popular indicator.

Bearish divergence signal

There is usually a negative alternative for each positive pattern, and this is also the case when it comes to divergence. When a market hits higher highs but does not follow the RSI, this is called "declining divergence" and can be a warning that a top is nearby. The following example is an hourly chart for the GBP / USD forex pair. As the blue and red arrows below show, the market was strong towards the middle of the month, but the RSI then reached a lower high than before, indicating that the momentum is starting to weaken.

This divergence approach using indicators is considered more reliable than using it as simple overbought or oversold signals. As always, nothing works all the time, but they can help measure the temperature of a market and serve as a warning that a previously good trend could be on the verge of coming to a standstill.

The wrong outbreak

As already mentioned, no trading strategy is always correct, but even wrong signals can give an indication of the market direction. The breakout strategy is very popular with momentum traders: if a previous low or high is broken on the chart, some see it as a sign of a new trend. But mostly that doesn't happen. This false breakout can still give us an aggressive trading strategy and is a useful technical analysis in itself.

The US 30 index chart shows this. The 17,900 level had served as support for a few days. The market then broke down but tried very quickly to regain its lost ground . There was no real tracking of the sale. An aggressive trading strategy would be to buy this strength with a stop loss order below the low after that support broke . Such false signals can become powerful. In this example, weak sellers were washed out and the market rose 150 points.

Support and resistance indicator
Support and resistance

The point at which a trend stops or pauses is support or resistance depending on the direction of movement. If it is not confined to a single point and reverses from a number of nearby points, it is a support zone or resistance zone. There is no standard indicator as a support and resistance indicator to identify the dynamic change in supply and demand. However, the functions of certain indicators can be extrapolated to a support and resistance indicator.

- support

Support is every price point that prevents the price from falling further. And depending on whether there is a temporary pause or a permanent reversal, the support defines its strength.

The demand is higher than the range of support.

In the USD / JPY hourly chart, support will be the point that acts as a demand zone and resumes the upward trend. The pair bounce off each base and create a new high that confirms the support.

How do I identify support?

Draw a straight line from the bearish reversal points.

If the line connects more than 3 reversal points, the line becomes a valid historical support.

This will become a critical point in the future as traders tend to use it as a reference for long trades.

In the EUR / GBP chart, the market is recovering from the same point, 0.83359 three times. This indicates strong demand for the asset. Indeed, these strong supports are the best entry points for long trades.

Support zone

It is not always possible for the market to recover from a single point every time. It bounces off points that are in the immediate vicinity of a wearer and converts it into a zone.

It is relatively difficult to cover the support zone in a short period of time. Longer periods of time can easily recognize the support zone.

The chart will be a weekly chart of EUR / USD. The pair does not find support as a point, but in a wide range of 1.03500 to 1.06000, becoming a zone.

In practice zones more than a point , as they are hard to break.

- resistance

Resistance is a point at which price action pauses or changes course during an increase.

The supply is more than the demand in the event of resistance.

On the EUR / CAD hourly chart, each time the pair pulls back, the supply-rich points that revive the downtrend are resistance. These points are good entry points for the short trade.

How do I identify resistance?

Draw a straight line connecting the reversal points.

If three or more dots kiss the line, it becomes resistance.

The frequency with which it was reversed is directly proportional to its strength.

Remember, when something happens twice, it's a coincidence, but when it happens three times, it becomes a pattern. And confirm it. The same applies to the trend line .

As indicated on the USD / CHF daily chart, point 1.00415 acts as a strong resistance. Every time it hits the 1.00415 mark, it acts as a wall and triggers a sharp downward movement.

Resistance zone

Similar to the support zone, the resistance zone identifies the group of resistance points in the midst of fluctuations and groups them into an area.

The reason why a number of points resist the price is incomprehensible.

Sometimes the fundamental factors also have a say. However, the occurrence in long-term charts is comparatively higher.

Support and resistance indicator (advanced methods)

The price action easily identifies the static supports and resistors. However, supply and demand vary dynamically at different times and at different times.

It is difficult to identify these supply and demand zones that support and resist price promotions using traditional methods. Indicators such as the moving average, Fibonacci tools and pivot points identify supply and demand zones at specific times and periods, depending on the trend, and are therefore referred to as support and resistance indicators .

Moving average as support

A moving average supports the price in many cases. It helps resume a trend after a correction in a directional movement. Therefore, the best starting points for a trend move are when prices are in the support zone around the moving averages.

In the graphic, the 100-SMA supports price movements and keeps the trend movement. Every time the price reaches the SMA, the trend revives. Or you can say that the moving average literally drives the price here.

Moving average as resistance

In a downtrend, moving averages resist pullback and serve as a vulnerable zone. They push the price down and maintain the bearish mood.

The zone in and around the 100-SMA resists retraction and continues the down-trend . In this case, the moving average acts as a resistance zone. And both SMA and EMA can play the role of support and resistance indicators. Learn more about the simple and exponential moving average, its application and strategies here.

Fibonacci retracement and extension

This is the best support and resistance indicator a trader can ask for. In an upward trend, the Fibonacci retracement points are the zones with strong demand, while the Fibonacci extension points are the supply zone (vice versa for the downward trend).

The Fibonacci retracement levels 0.236, 0.382, 0.5, 0.618 are strong supports with every directional movement. Depending on the type of trend, they act as a good supply or demand zone. Likewise, the Fibonacci expansions, in particular the 1.618 point (in an upward trend), support or support (in a downward trend) the price movement. People (traders are people too) tend to respond to Fibonacci values, and this psychologically plays a big role in a trader's decision making.

The table of GBY/JPY can be a good example that the Fibonacci indicator is a support and resistance indicator. The

GBP / JPY pair is retreating in a downtrend. The retracement value of 0.5 from the previous trend movement strongly resists the price movement. It limits the price and sends it down. Extension point 1.618 also maintains the falling price.

Both points were not significant points based on previous price promotions. But there has been considerable courtesy of Fibonacci numbers. Learn more about Fibonacci numbering in Elliott Wave here .

Pivot point

The pivot is the best intraday support and resistance indicator. It shows the supports and resistances for the day based on the movement of the previous day. If you are an intraday trader, these values are vital for you.

Role reversal - perfect way to exchange support and resistance

Whenever the support is interrupted, it resists the price action. Resistance also maintains price movement when prices break through. Experienced trades use these role change instances to validate the breakout.

So don't initiate trading as soon as support or resistance breaks.

Wait until the price action has withdrawn or set back to the same level. Then initiate a trade.

It reduces your risk and avoids falling. Therefore, it is undoubtedly the best entry point.

For example, point 0.90013 initially opposes the price action. Once the pair breaks the 0.90013 resistance and crosses it will transform into a supply zone.

Do you want to see reversals? Here is a modern harmonic pattern - the dragon pattern here .

The central theses

The demand-facing zone supports an asset. The supply-rich zone also opposes the price movement.

The zones are stronger than a point.

The strength of the support and resistance zone is directly proportional to the frequency of the reversal.

Moving averages, Fibonacci retracements and extensions can be extrapolated as support and resistance indicators.

One breakthrough or resistance turns into another when it breaks through. It is the best place to start a trade.

Types of support and resistance lines

There are many types of support and resistance levels on the market. They differ in the way they are formed. The following list shows some of the most important levels that every trader should know.

1) Horizontal support and resistance levels

Horizontal support and resistance levels are the most basic type of these levels. They are simply identified by a horizontal line. First of all, you need to recognize a past price level where the price had difficulty breaking above or below. Then mark it with a horizontal line that shines into the future. As soon as the price approaches this horizontal line again, there is a high probability that the price will decrease from this line.

2) Round number support and resistance levels

Another type of support and resistance levels are round number levels that are built around round exchange rates. These levels of support and resistance are psychological levels. Since market participants tend to base their stop levels or profit targets on round numbers, the number of market orders increases by these levels.

Support and resistance levels for round numbers are horizontal lines drawn at exchange rates for round numbers such as 1.00, 1.10, 1.20, 1.25, etc. The graph will show the EUR / USD pair, with each round number acting as a resistance and support line.

3) Trend line support and resistance levels

Trend line support and resistance levels are not drawn by horizontal lines, but by trend lines that can be inclined up or down. Since the forex market likes to be trending, trend lines are often used to identify up and down trends.

Every time the price approaches a trend line, there is a high probability that the price will bounce off the trend line. As with horizontal support and resistance levels, the trendline should touch at least three price points before it is considered important.

Similar to trend lines, channels can also be used to identify support and resistance levels. A channel offers both support and resistance for the price through its lower channel line or upper channel line. The following diagram shows a support and resistance diagram based on a rising channel.

4) Fibonacci support and resistance levels

The Fibonacci retracement tool is an extremely popular tool for determining price levels at which a price correction could end. This leads to the continuation of the underlying trend. Price corrections are opposing price movements during up and down trends, which give price charts their characteristic zigzag pattern.

Leonardo Fibonacci was a famous Italian mathematician from the Middle Ages who is known for the following Fibonacci number sequence: 1,1,2,3,5,8,13,21,34 ... If you divide a number in a row With his successor you always get the same result: 0.618. This ratio, also known as the golden ratio, is widespread in nature and naturally also occurs in the human body.

Market participants believe that the golden ratio can be used to measure the extent of price corrections in the market. The 61.8% Fibonacci retracement is believed to be an important support for the price. In any case, practice shows that the market tends to respect the 61.8% Fib retracement, including other variations in Fibonacci ratios. The following table shows an example of how Fibonacci retracement levels are used to identify support levels.

5) Dynamic support and resistance levels
As the name suggests, dynamic support and resistance levels change with each new price tick. To achieve dynamic levels of support and resistance, traders typically use moving averages that are automatically pulled from your trading platform. The 200-day exponential moving average (EMA), the 100-day EMA, and the 50-day EMA are very popular dynamic support and resistance levels.

Choosing the best technical indicators

To find the best technical indicators for your particular day trading approach, test some of them individually and then in combination. You may stay at four, which are evergreen, or switch off depending on the asset you are trading or the market conditions of the day.

Regardless of whether you are day trading stocks, forex or futures, it is often best to keep the technical indicators simple. You may prefer to look at just two indicators to suggest entry and exit points. Use at most one indicator from each category of indicators to avoid unnecessary and distracting repetitions.

Combine day trading indicators

Consider combining sets of two indicators in your price chart to identify points that can be initiated to exit a trade. For example, RSI and moving average convergence / divergence can be combined on the screen to propose and amplify a trading signal.

The relative strength index (RSI) is at overbought

or oversold conditions indicate, by the price dynamics measures an asset. The indicator was created by J. Welles Wilder Jr., who pointed out that the dynamic of 30 (on a scale from 0 to 100) was a sign that an asset was oversold - and therefore a buying opportunity - and a 70- Percentage level was a sign of an asset that was overbought - and thus a sale or short sale opportunity. Constance Brown, CMT, refined the use of the index, saying that the oversold level in an upward market was actually much higher than 30 and the oversold level in a downward market was much lower than 70.

Using the Wilder levels, the asset price may continue to rise for some time, while the RSI indicates overbought, and vice versa. For this reason, RSI is best tracked only if its signal matches the price trend: for example, look for bearish momentum signals when the price trend is bearish and ignore these signals when the price trend is bullish.

To make it easier to spot these price trends, you can use the moving average convergence / divergence (MACD) indicator. MACD consists of two diagram lines. The MACD line is generated by subtracting an exponential moving average (EMA) with 26 periods from an EMA with 12 periods. An EMA is the average price of an asset over a period of time, with the only difference that the most recent prices are weighted more than the more distant prices.

The second line is the signal line and a 9-period EMA. A bearish trend is signaled when the MACD line falls below the signal line; An upward trend is signaled when the MACD line crosses the signal line.

Select pairs

When choosing pairs, it is advisable to choose an indicator that serves as a leading indicator (like RSI) and as a lag indicator (like MACD). Leading indicators generate signals before the conditions for entry into the trade are created. Trailing indicators generate signals after these conditions occur, so they serve as confirmation of leading indicators and can prevent you from trading in the wrong signals. [5]

You should also choose a pair that includes indicators from two of the four different types, never two of the same type. The four types are trend (like MACD), momentum (like RSI), volatility and volume. As the name suggests, volatility indicators are based on the volatility of the asset price and volume indicators on the trading volume of the asset. It is generally not helpful to observe two indicators of the same type because they provide the same information.

Use multiple indicators

You can also choose to have an indicator for each type on the screen, two of which may be leading and two may be delayed. Several indicators can amplify trading signals even more and increase the likelihood of sorting out wrong signals.

Refinement indicators

Regardless of what indicators you graph, you should analyze them and make notes of their effectiveness over time. Ask yourself: What are the disadvantages of an indicator? Does it generate a lot of wrong signals? Can't it signal what leads to missed opportunities? Does it signal too early (more likely for an early indicator) or too late (more likely for a lagging)?

An indicator may be effective when trading stocks but not, for example, forex. You may want to swap one indicator for another of its type or make changes to the calculation. Such refinements are an essential part of success in day-to-day trading in technical indicators.

INTRODUCTION TO SWING TRADING

The forex market is the most significant financial market on the planet, with the details going a lengthy method to back that up. During April 2016, records show that, on average, $5.1 trillion was traded every day. What you can likewise take from this is precisely how well-known forex trading has become, with this figure introducing an outstanding bounce on the $4 trillion posted, on average, every day during April 2010. With an ever-increasing number of individuals participating in forex trading, than at any other time, we hear unlimited anecdotes about traders getting their fingers copied. The purposes behind this are quite clear; the same number of traders don't comprehend the forex market; they commit similar errors on numerous occasions.

As we would see it, most traders lose money since they just have no genuine handle of the 10,000-foot view. Comprehend that the initial 6 to a year of forex trading can be fantastically overwhelming, with possible losses and entanglements apparently around each turn. Helping you to evade those entanglements, address the primary motivation why you may be losing money, and set you back destined for success to forex trading achievement, the accompanying data is something that you are going to need to focus on memory.

Swing trading has been depicted as a sort of central trading in which positions are held for longer than a single day. Most fundamentalists are swing traders since changes in corporate basics by and large require a few days or even seven days to make adequate price development render a reasonable profit.

However, this depiction of swing trading is an improvement. In all actuality, swing trading sits in the continuum between day trading to slant trading. A day trader will hold a stock anyplace from a couple of moments to a couple of hours; however, never over a day, a pattern trader looks at the long-term central patterns of a stock or file and may hold the stock for half a month or months. Swing traders hold a specific stock for a while, by and large, a couple of days to a little while, which is between those boundaries, and they will trade the stock based on its intra-week or intra-month motions among good faith and cynicism. Notes:

•   Most fundamentalists are swing traders since changes in corporate basics by and large require a few days or even seven days to make adequate price development render a reasonable profit.

•   Swing trading sits in the continuum between day trading to drift trading.

•   The first key to fruitful swing trading is picking the correct stocks.

Swing trading is a pattern of trading that endeavors to catch short-to-medium-term gains in a stock (or any financial instrument) over a time of a couple of days to a little while. Swing traders fundamentally utilize specialized investigation to search for trading openings. These traders may use essential examination notwithstanding investigating price patterns and patterns.

- Swing trading includes making trades that last two or three days as long as a while to profit from a foreseen price move.

- Swing trading opens a trader to expedite and end of the week risk, where the price could hole and open the accompanying the meeting at a significantly excellent price.

- Swing traders can take profits using a growing risk/reward proportion dependent on a stop loss and profit target, or they can take profits or losses dependent on a specific marker or price action developments.

Swing trading helps me to remember staying on the shore of a sea, watching the waves. Each wave has a peak and trough—a swing from high to low or low to high that copies the all-over the movement of stocks. Swing traders don't attempt to ride that wave by riding close to the peak, yet by cruising their boat from trough to peak like in film scenes.

There are two sorts of swing trading styles. The first is to extend trade, that is, buy and sell as price skips between a low and significant expense. If you realize what a square shape chart pattern is or a channel, at that point, you can buy close to the base and sell close to the top more than once. I find that the profit capability of range trading isn't energizing enough for me.

• Range trading is buying and selling as price skips among highs and lows.

I like to get a swing when it starts and hold it until it closes. It is a similar thought as a range trade, yet the high–low range is frequently a lot bigger (if you are fortunate), and you just trade it once.

- A pattern trade buys close to the swing low and sells close to the furthest limit of a short-term pattern (or the converse: sell high and buy low).

Swing trading is attempting to get the price as it moves among pinnacles and valleys. Another approach to state this swing trading is catching the move between layers of help and obstruction.

Swing trading focus around medium-term investment methodologies and endeavours to make profits when the stock goes up and when it descends – consequently, the expression "swing." This sort of investment strategy – regarding the longevity of trade – sits someplace in the middle of day trading and buy-and-hold contributing.

Day trading is the most theoretical of the investment methodologies where stock is held for short of what one day, here and there for just a couple of hours or minutes, even seconds. Day traders profit by short-term moves in resources – selling at a certain pre-characterized level to stay away from the risk of counter moves during out-of-hours trade.

Buy-and-hold – or pattern contributing – is a long-term strategy, where financial specialists follow a specific pattern: maybe a repeating rally to profit by ascends in stocks most firmly united to a fortifying worldwide economy, or maybe a "development" strategy concentrating on those stocks that deliver the highest profits.

Inside Swing Trading

Swing trading is a medium-term strategy – as a rule over a couple of days, up to around three weeks – where the financial specialist follows flooding and blurring fortunes of a benefit or resources, putting resources into both the additions and the losses.

Monetary markets never go one way always, and by having the option to exploit that, you can expand your profits as you in principle will be bringing in money when the market ascends throughout the following barely any days, and afterwards make some when the market pulls back, as it will unquestionably do at some point or another.

Having the option to detect the turnarounds is significant, and specialized examination will have the option to help here. Yet, the best guide to this kind of investment strategy is a market that is going no place. A range-bound market has been demonstrating similar patterns for a little while. No stuns, for example, surprising loan cost moves, or market mediation by money related specialists.

Regarding cooperation, swing trading is likewise progressively adjusted between the full-time interest paces of day traders and afterwardss contribute and hold up of pattern contributing, so experts can hold an all-day work while taking part in swing trading.

Swing Trading

Everybody needs to distinguish swing trading systems that work. If solitary, it was that simple. Looking back, the stock market adjustment, for the most part, gave some great conditions to a swing trading strategy, albeit unstable markets are bound to neutralize swing trading (see "burdens" underneath). An adjustment is a point at which an advantage, file, or other price marker falls over 10% from its latest repetitive pinnacle.

Picking the stocks to follow was not troublesome, given the broad understanding that innovation stocks were among the most exaggerated. During the revision, the S&P 500 innovation segment fell by 10.4%. Vitality stocks, demonstrated the most exceedingly awful performing area during the remedy as oil prices likewise experienced their downturn.

The swing trader would not have been probably going to get the entirety of the drawback, yet the signs that an amendment was in progress would before the long rise. It would have been getting the upside after the adjustment finished that represented the most troublesome issue in market timing.

The best swing trading systems include the broad utilization of specialized trading procedures. Many utilize charting instruments, for example, exponential moving averages (EMA), oscillators, and fractals. For traders hoping to trade with swings, or traders hoping to extend their ID of market swings, the fractal pointer can be of extraordinary help.

Understanding Swing Trading

Typically, swing trading includes holding a position either long or short for more than one trading meeting, however typically not longer than a little while or two or three months. This is a general period, as certain trades may last longer than several months, yet the trader may at present think of them as swing trades. Swing traders can likewise happen during a trading meeting. However, this is a surprising result that is realized by very unpredictable conditions.

The objective of swing trading is to catch a lump of a potential price move. While a few traders search out unpredictable stocks with bunches of development, others may lean toward progressively steady stocks. In either case, swing trading is the way toward recognizing where a benefit's price is probably going to move straightaway, entering a position, and afterwards catching a lump of the profit if that move emerges. Fruitful swing traders are just hoping to catch a lump of the normal price move and afterwards proceed onward to the following chance.

This is one of the most popular types of dynamic trading, where traders search for the middle of the road term openings utilizing different types of specialized investigation. In case you're keen on swing trading, you ought to be personally acquainted with the specialized examination. Specialized Analysis Course gives an exhaustive outline of the subject with more than five hours of on-request video, works out, and natural substance spread both fundamental and propelled procedures.

Many swing traders survey trades on a risk/reward premise. By dissecting the chart of an advantage, they figure out where they will enter, where they will put a stop loss, and afterward envision where they can get out with a profit. Suppose they are risking $1 per share on an arrangement that could sensibly deliver a $3 gain, which is a great risk/reward. Then again, risking $1 to make $1 or just make $0.75 isn't exactly as good.

Swing traders principally utilize specialized investigation because of the short-term nature of the trades. The basic investigation can be utilized to upgrade the examination. For instance, if a swing trader sees a bullish arrangement in stock, they might need to confirm that the basics of the advantage look good or are improving too.

Swing traders will frequently search for circumstances on the day by day outlines and may watch 1-hour or 15-minute graphs to discover exact entry, stop loss, and take profit levels.

Merits

• Requires less an ideal opportunity to trade than day trading

• Maximizes short-term profit potential by catching the majority of market swings

• Traders can depend solely on specialized examination, rearranging the trading procedure

Demerits

• Trade positions are dependent upon overnight and end of the week market risk

- Abrupt market inversions can bring about considerable losses
- Swing traders frequently miss longer-term patterns for short-term market moves

Day Trading versus Swing Trading

The qualification between swing trading and day trading is, normally, the holding time for positions. Swing trading frequently, includes a short-term hold, while day traders finish off positions before the market closes. To sum up, day trading positions are constrained to a single day while swing trading includes holding for a few days to weeks.

By holding, for the time being, the swing trader causes the unconventionality of overnight risk, for example, holes up or against the position. By taking on the overnight risk, swing trades are normally finished with a littler position size contrasted with day trading (accepting the two traders have likewise measured records). Day traders normally use bigger position estimates and may utilize a day trading edge of 25%.

Swing traders additionally approach edge or influence of half. This implies if the trader is affirmed for edge trading, they just need to set up $25,000 in the capital for a trade with a current estimation of $50,000, for instance.

Swing Trading Tactics

A swing trader will, in a general search for multi-day chart patterns. A portion of the more typical patterns includes moving average hybrids, cup-and-handle patterns, head and shoulders patterns, banners, and triangles. Key inversion candles might be utilized, notwithstanding different markers, to devise a strong trading plan.

Eventually, each swing trader devises an arrangement and strategy that gives them an edge over numerous trades. This includes searching for trade arrangements that will, in general, lead to unsurprising developments in the advantage's price. This isn't simple, and no strategy or arrangement works unfailingly. With an ideal risk/reward, winning each time isn't required. The greater the risk/compensation of a trading strategy, the fewer occasions it needs to win to deliver an overall profit over numerous trades.

The Right Stocks for Swing Trading

The best up-and-comers are huge top stocks, which are among the most effectively traded stocks on the significant trades. In a functioning market, these stocks will swing between comprehensively characterized high and low limits, and the swing trader will ride the wave one way for two or three days or weeks just to change to the contrary side of the trade when the stock turns around heading.

The Right Market

In both of the two market limits, the bear market condition or seething buyer market, swing trading ends up being a preferably extraordinary test over in a market between these two boundaries. In these boundaries, even the most dynamic stocks won't show the equivalent here and their motions as when records are moderately steady for half a month or months. In a bear market or buyer market, the force will, by and large, convey stocks for a long timeframe one way in particular, subsequently affirming that the best strategy is to trade based on the longer-term directional pattern.

The swing trader, in this way, is best positioned when markets are going no place – when records ascend for a few days, at that point decrease for the following barely any days, just to rehash a similar general pattern and once more. Two or three months may go with significant stocks and records generally at a similar spot as their levels. However, the swing trader has had numerous chances to get the short-term developments all over (in some cases inside a channel).

The issue with both swing trading and long-term pattern trading is that achievement depends on effectively distinguishing what kind of market is as of now being experienced. Pattern trading would have been the perfect strategy for the positively trending market of the last 50% of the 1990s, while swing trading likely would have been best for 2000 and 2001.

Utilizing the Exponential Moving Average

Straightforward moving averages (SMAs) offer help and obstruction levels, just as bullish and bearish patterns. Backing and obstruction levels can flag whether to buy a stock. Bullish and bearish hybrid patterns signal price focuses where you ought to enter and exit stocks.

The exponential moving average (EMA) is a variety of the SMA that places more accentuation on the most recent information focuses. The EMA gives traders clear pattern signs, and entry and exit focus quicker than a basic moving average. The EMA hybrid can be utilized in swing trading to time entry and exit focuses.

An essential EMA hybrid framework can be utilized by concentrating on the nine-, 13-and 50-period EMAs. A bullish hybrid happens when the price crosses over these moving averages in the wake of being underneath. This implies an inversion might be likely to work out and that an upswing might be starting. At the instance when the nine-time frame EMA crosses over the 13-time frame EMA, it flags a long entry. However, the 13-time frame EMA must be over the 50-time frame EMA or cross above it.

Then again, a bearish hybrid happens when the price of a security falls underneath these EMAs. This signals a possible inversion of a pattern, and it very well may be utilized to time an exit of a long position. At the instance when the nine-time frame EMA crosses beneath the 13-time frame EMA, it flags a short entry or an exit of a long position. However, the 13-time frame EMA needs to underneath the 50-time frame EMA or cross beneath it.

The Baseline

Much exploration of chronicled information has demonstrated that, in a market helpful for swing trading, liquid stocks will in general trade above and under gauge esteem, which is depicted on an outline with an EM). An enormous number of traders utilize the comprehension of a stock's conduct above and beneath the benchmark to portray the swing trader's strategy of "buying commonality and selling craziness" or "shorting regularity and covering wretchedness." Once the swing trader has utilized the EMA to distinguish the normal gauge on the stock graph, the person goes long at the standard when the stock is going up and short at the pattern when the stock is on its way down.

In this way, swing traders are not hoping to hit the grand slam with a solitary trade – they are not worried about the ideal chance to buy a stock precisely at its base and sell precisely at its top (or the other way around). In an ideal trading condition, they trust that the stock will hit its gauge and affirm its bearing before they make their moves. The story gets increasingly entangled when a more grounded upswing or downtrend is affecting everything: the trader may incomprehensibly go long when the stock plunges underneath its EMA and trust that the stock will return up in an uptrend, or the person may short a stock that has cut over the EMA and sit tight for it to drop if the longer pattern is down.

Taking Profits

At the instance when it comes time to take profits, the swing trader will need to exit the trade as close as conceivable to the upper or lower channel line without being excessively exact, which may cause the risk of passing up on the best chance. In a solid market, when a stock is showing a solid directional pattern, traders can hang tight for the channel

line to be reached before taking their profit; however, in a more fragile market, they may take their profits before the line is hit (if the heading changes and the line doesn't get hit on that specific swing).
Swing trading is extraordinary compared to other trading styles for the starting trader to get their feet wet. However, despite everything offered the noteworthy profit potential for the middle of the road and propelled traders. Swing traders get adequate input on their trades following a few days to keep them inspired; however, their long and short positions of a few days are of the term that doesn't prompt distraction.

On the other hand, pattern trading offers more prominent profit potential if a trader can get a significant market pattern of weeks or months. Yet, few are the traders with adequate order to hold a position that long without getting occupied. Then again, trading many stocks every (day trading) may simply demonstrate too white-knuckle of a ride for a few, making swing trading the ideal medium between the boundaries.

Points of interest and Disadvantages of Swing Trading

How about we look at the favourable circumstances and weaknesses of swing trading.

Focal points

• Markets never go a similar way constantly, and swing trading permits the speculator to exploit this, expanding likely returns by sponsorship the meeting and the pullback

• It's not a full-time interest: not at all like day trading, where you should be on the head of every one of your trades each moment, with swing trading, you loosen up somewhat more as you've set your investment to run through the span of a few days. You can swing trade while continuing with an all-day work

• It's likewise less capital concentrated. You may have a few trades going on simultaneously. However, you're not continually in the market like day traders and thinking of new edge for new positions, or have a great deal of capital tied up over a long period like buy-and-hold financial specialists

• Bad trades can be constrained. Utilizing the specialized fitting signs, you should know when a trade isn't working all the more rapidly and breaking point the harm is done

Weaknesses

• Market instability. Unstable markets are not the best conditions in which to work on swing trading in such a case that you get the signs off-base, all past profit can be cleared out very quickly

• Similarly, you can't generally confide in your intuition following the patterns. While markets frequently show extensive times of range-bound trading, they are whimsical, and you should not accept that the help and obstruction levels you've distinguished will hold today

• Using fractals isn't sufficient. You should be appropriately fixed on specialized examination to make this work, and that implies the study

• It's distressing. Possibly not as brazen as day trading, however, you've despite everything got the opportunity to have a cool and considered outlook that is not inclined to be frightened without any problem

This isn't the strategy for everybody. Indeed, even some buy-and-hold financial specialists get frightened when the market is in unrest, yet they realize that if it's a decent resource, it will rebound back and keep on bringing in money for them. The more regularly you are in the market, the more probable it is you're going to commit an error. Become accustomed to losses, since you will have ineffective trades. Indeed, even the most learned systematic financial specialists can't be correct constantly. This goes twofold for day traders.

What Exactly Is Swing Trading?

Swing trading is a trade-off between standard long term pattern trading and your run of the mill day trading. If you are pattern trading, you are generally inspired by different crucial patterns for an individual stock or a file that keeps going for longer measures of time. These sorts of traders hold on to a stock for at any rate a little while to even a while. Day traders are the contrary outrageous of the range. They hold on to stocks or lists for anyplace from minor seconds to even a few hours, yet they strictly close out their positions around the same time. Framework based swing traders rather buy a stock for a medium time span. This may be from a couple of days to half a month. Your objective in swing trading is to trade these stocks dependent on varieties of the week after week or month to month lows to highs.

The Best Market for Practicing Swing Trading

There are two specific sorts of markets where swing trading doesn't work so well. It ends up being difficult to be effective at it if the market is in a seething buyer market or a plunging bear market. In either case, it is difficult to profit from here and their fluctuation in a given stock. The explanation is because in bull or bear markets, stocks by and large move firmly for expanded timeframes either an upward or descending way.

Swing traders are at their absolute best in an inside and out of the aimless market. The market you need as a swing trader is sideways. In this kind of market, the trades may go up for a couple of days and afterwards return for a few trading meetings. The pattern rehashes itself and once more. The final product of trading in a sideways market is that the records would wind up at about the level they started. This is actually what swing traders need. They are searching for all the potential open doors they can discover to take an interest in here and there moves that happen over the short term.

This makes the most troublesome piece of swing trading effectively, knowing the sort of market that is in progress at some random point. You need to consider the vital records' extents to decide whether they are limited in the upper protections and lower underpins, which the markets built up through the span of a while. Swing trading will keep on being perfect until the market files make a considerable break out to the base or top.

The Best Type of Swing Trading Stocks

It makes sense that there are stocks that loan themselves preferable to swing trading over others. The best up-and-comers have ended up being the enormous top stocks of significant organizations that additionally happen to be the most vigorously traded protections. Exploration has that these sorts of stocks swing from demonstrated highs to lows in markets that are trading sideways. You can exploit this pattern to ride the stock in the at present moving bearing as long as it proceeds for a couple of days or once in a while weeks. At the instance, when it switches heading, you can essentially finish off the position and go in on the contrary side to ride it the other way.

Strategy for Swing Trading

With swing trading, you start with a strategy to gain proficiency with the stock's standard worth. You can see this on graphs by pulling up exponential moving averages. Because of EMAs, swing traders know about the level to sell a stock short as it descends past the benchmark. They likewise understand this is the ideal level to buy the stock when it climbs past it. The objective with swing trading isn't to catch huge increases in a single trade. It additionally isn't basic to ride the entire movie from the pattern to the base or the top. Traders rehearsing this strategy are watching stock and hanging tight for it to affirm its bearing after it hits the gauge. The idea has a few varieties if the market is unequivocally slanting to the upside. In these cases, if the stock price decreases underneath the EMA, you could take a long position with the thought it would bounce back a while later. It is the equivalent of firmly declining markets. At the instance, when the stock price climbs past the EMA, you may short the stock and hang tight for it to move down. Understand that these minor departure from swing trading involve risks, since the strategy truly works best with sideways trading markets.

Swing Trading and Profit Taking Swing traders might want to capitalize on trade as close as possible to the upper or lower channel lines of the stock. These channel lines are essentially the help and opposition levels that contain the stock trading extent to the base and the top. Normally no swing trader is going to catch the entirety of out of here each event. If you are too hungry, it might be counterproductive. You may wind up acknowledging less of the move whenever it inverts and pass up the opportunity to ride the stock the other heading as it moves back toward the EMA benchmark.

SWING TRADING BASICS: WHAT IT IS AND HOW IT WORKS

The way toward swing exchanging has turned into a well-known stock exchanging technique utilized by numerous dealers over the market. This style of exchanging has demonstrated to be exceptionally effective for some dedicated stocks and Forex dealers. Customarily swing exchanging has been characterized as a progressively theoretical methodology as the positions are generally purchased and held for the dealers foreordained time allotment. These time allotments could run somewhere in the range of two days to a couple of months. The objective of the swing broker is to distinguish the pattern either up or and place their exchanges in the most invaluable position. From that point, the trader will ride the pattern to what they decide as to the depletion point and sell for a benefit. Intermittently swing brokers will use a wide range of specialized markers that will enable them to have a progressively good likelihood when making their exchanges. Shorter-term brokers don't in general swing exchange as they lean toward holding positions for the day and practising them preceding the end of the market. Swing exchanging technique uses time, and it is this time is the impediment factor for long time dealers. Generally, there is a lot of hazards associated with the end of the market and that a trader won't acknowledge this hazard.

Swing exchanging is a style of exchanging that endeavours to catch increases a stock (or any monetary instrument) over a time of a couple of days to a little while. Swing brokers principally utilize specialized investigation to search for exchanging openings. These brokers may use principal examination notwithstanding breaking value patterns and examples

Swing exchanging is a more extended term exchanging style that expects persistence to hold your exchanges for a few days one after another. It is perfect for the individuals who can't screen their outlines for the day; however,they can devote two or three hours examining the market each night.

This is likely most appropriate for the individuals who have all day employments or school yet have enough extra time to keep awake-to-date with what is happening in the worldwide economies.

Swing exchanging endeavours to recognize "swings" inside a medium-term pattern and enter just when there is by all accounts a high likelihood of winning.

For instance, in an upturn, you intend to purchase (go long) at "swing lows." And on the other hand, sell (go short) at "swing highs" to exploit transitory countertrends.

Since exchanges last any longer than one day, bigger stop misfortunes are required to climate instability, and a forex trader must adjust that to their cash the board plan.

You will, in all likelihood, observe exchanges conflict with you during the holding time since there can be numerous variances of the value during the shorter periods.

Significantly, you can try to avoid panicking during these occasions and trust in your examination.

Since exchanges more often than not have bigger targets, spreads won't have as quite a bit of an effect on your general benefits.

Thus, exchanging sets with bigger spreads and lower liquidity is worthy.

You should be a swing dealer if:

You wouldn't fret holding your exchanges for a few days.

You are eager to take fewer exchanges, however progressively cautious, to ensure your exchanges are generally excellent arrangements.

You wouldn't fret having enormous stop misfortunes.

You are understanding.

You can resist the urge to panic when exchanges move against you.

You might NOT have any desire to be a swing dealer if:

You like quick-paced, and activity stuffed exchanging.

You are fretful and like to know whether you are correct or wrong right away.

You get sweat-soaked and on edge when exchanges conflict with you.

You can't put in two or three hours consistently to break the business sectors.

You can't surrender your World of Warcraft striking sessions.

The differentiation of swing exchanging is an expansive point in that it has various impacts from a huge number of various exchanging procedures. These exchanging procedures are interesting and have their particular hazard profiles. Swing exchanging can be a great path for a market member to improve their specialized investigation abilities further while allowing them a chance to give more consideration to the first site of the exchange. Numerous fruitful swing brokers have been into utilizing a Bollinger band procedure as an apparatus to help them in entering and leaving positions. For a swing dealer to be fruitful at the methodology, they should have a high bent for deciding the present market pattern and putting their situations as per that pattern. It does a swing dealer note great to put a short position with the arrangement of holding for an all-inclusive timeframe in a market that is slanting upwards. The general subject here is that the objective of the dealers ought to be to build their likelihood of progress while restricting or wiping out hazard-totally. The swing dealer's most noticeably awful foe is that of a sideways or in a dynamic market. Sideways value activity will stop a swing trader cold in their tracks as there is no overall pattern to key off of.

At the point when utilized effectively, swing exchanging is a superb system utilized by numerous traders crosswise over various markets. It isn't just utilized in the Forex showcase; however, it is a key apparatus in fates and value markets. Swing dealers take the abilities that they learn through specialized examination and can even parlay these aptitudes into different alternative techniques. The transient idea of swing exchanging separates it from that of the conventional speculator. Speculators will, in general, have a more extended term time skyline and are not customarily influenced by momentary value variances. As usual, one must recollect that swing exchanging is just a single technique and ought to be used just when properly comprehended. Like any exchanging system, swing exchanging can be unsafe, and preservationist methodologies can transform into day exchanging procedures rapidly. If you intend to utilize a swing exchanging system, guarantee that you completely comprehend the dangers and build up a technique that will have the option to enable you to produce the greatest rate returns on your positions.

Swing exchanging is one of exchanging styles which generally executed in theoretical action in monetary markets, for example, securities, item, foreign trade, stock, and stock record. Normally this exchanging style requires a swing dealer to hold their exchanging position more than one exchanging day, generally 2 to 5 exchanging days. Swing exchanging is mainstream in exchanging world as this exchanging styles, for the most part, has a decent hazard and reward proportion, it implies the likelihood to pick up benefit is greater than the hazard that may ascend in each exchange.

By and large, swing exchanging goes for 100 pips benefit likelihood. Benefit potential can be picked up from each market swing. A swing broker, particularly in foreign trade and stock file advertise, can go both long or short of accepting each open door. It likewise implies, inside an exchanging week, when a market is unpredictable, a swing dealer may run over a few exchanging openings the individual in question can take.

Contrasted with scalping exchanging or day exchanging, clearly swing exchanging has less exchanging chances, notwithstanding, as should be obvious here if you execute this exchanging style, most likely you will have more opportunity to do your different exercises as you don't need to keep your eyes on a market all the exchanging day. You will just get fewerchances, however, with a high likelihood of winning for every chance. It is your call to pick which exchanging style to apply. No exchanging style is immaculate, and there is constantly in addition to and short.

Presently, if you surely need to give an attempt to swing exchanging, you can discover a few procedures from numerous assets accessible on the web. You may discover a few books and some other instructive materials on swing exchanging. You can visit and be an individual from some exchanging discussions too. Notwithstanding, as regular, I need to advise you that there are likewise some shifty individuals guaranteeing themselves as swing exchanging masters; however, they simply need you to purchase their refuse training materials. Simply be mindful of such individuals.

Luckily, in the wake of getting some essential comprehension and experience on swing exchanging, you can be a decent swing trader also. You can even think of your swing exchanging systems. Numerous individuals appreciate the advantage of building up their swing exchanging systems as they are the main ones who realize their exchanging character, need, and style. Never quit to figure out how to be a decent swing trader, even though unquestionably, it will require some investment to ace swing exchanging brilliantly. Yet, at last, the majority of your endeavours will payout.

Issues With Swing Trading Using Options

Swing exchanging is one of the most widely recognized methods for exchanging the securities exchange. You presumably have been swing exchanging all these while. Swing exchanging is purchasing every so often selling a couple of days or weeks after the fact when costs are higher, or lower (on account of a short). Such a cost increment or lessening is known a "Value Swing," subsequently the expression "Swing Trading."

Most learners to choices exchanging take up choices as a type of influence for their swing exchanging. They need to purchase call choices when costs are low and afterwards rapidly sell them a couple of days or weeks after the fact for a utilized addition. The other way around valid for put choices. In any case, many such amateurs immediately discovered the most difficult way possible that in choices swing exchanging, and they could, in any case, make a generous misfortune regardless of whether the stock inevitably moved toward the path that they anticipated.

How is that so? What are a few issues related to swing exchanging utilizing alternatives that they neglected to observe?

For sure, even though choices can be utilized just as utilized substitution for exchanging the basic stock, there are a couple of things about alternatives that most tenderfoots neglect to observe.

1) Strike Price

It doesn't take long for anybody to understand that there are numerous alternatives accessible crosswise over many strike costs for every single optionable stock. The undeniable decision that fledgelings generally make is to purchase the "modest" out of the cash alternatives for greater influence. Out of the cash, choices are alternatives that have no work in an incentive in them. These are called alternatives with strike costs higher than the overarching stock cost or put choices with strike costs lower than the overall stock cost.

The issue with purchasing out of the cash alternatives in swing exchanging is that regardless of whether the basic stock move toward your expectation (upwards for purchasing call choices and downwards for purchasing put choices), you could at present lose ALL your cash if the stock didn't surpass the strike cost of the choices you purchased! The truth is out; this is known as "Lapse Out Of The Money," which makes every one of the choices you purchased useless. This is likewise how most fledgelings lose all their cash in choices exchanging.

By and large, the more out of the cash the choices are, the higher the influence, and the higher the hazard that those alternatives will terminate useless, losing all of you the cash put into them. The more in cash the choices are, the lower increasingly costly they are because of the worth incorporated with them; the lower the influence turns out to be nevertheless the lower the danger of terminating useless. You have to take the normal extent of the move and the measure of hazard you can mull over when choosing which strike cost to purchase for swing exchanging with choices. If you anticipate a major move, out of the cash choices would give you huge rewards, yet if the move neglects to surpass the strike cost of those choices by termination, a terrible arousing is standing by.

2) Expiration Date

Not at all like swing exchanging with stocks which you can clutch never-ending when things turn out badly, alternatives have a distinct lapse date. This implies if you are incorrect, you will rapidly lose cash when lapse lands without the advantage of having the option to clutch the position and hang tight for arrival or profit.

Indeed, swing exchanging with choices is battling against time. The quicker the stock moves, the more sure you are of benefit. The uplifting news is, all optionable stocks have choices crosswise over numerous termination months too. Closer month choices are less expensive, and further month alternatives are progressively costly. All things considered, if you are sure that the hidden stock is going to move rapidly, you could exchange with closer termination month alternatives or what we call "Front Month Options," which are less expensive and subsequently have a greater influence.

Real-World Example of Swing Trade in Apple

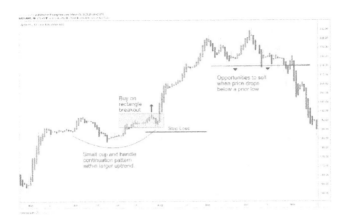

The diagram above demonstrates a period where Apple (AAPL) had a solid value move higher. This was trailed by a little cup and handle design, which frequently flags a continuation of the value rise if the stock moves over the high of the handle.

For this situation, the cost rises over the handle, setting off a conceivable purchase close $192.70.

One conceivable spot to put a stop misfortune is beneath the handle, set apart by the square shape, close $187.50.

Because of the section and stop misfortune, the evaluated hazard for the exchange is $5.20 per share ($192.70 - $187.50).

If searching for a potential reward that is in any event double the hazard, any cost above $203.10 ($192.70 +(2 *$5.20)) will give this.

Besides a hazard/remunerates, the trader could likewise use other leave techniques, for example, trusting that the cost will make an extraordinary failure. With this strategy, a left sign wasn't given until $216.46, when the value dipped under the earlier pullback low. This strategy would have brought about a benefit of $23.76 per share. Thought of another way: a 12% benefit in return for under 3% chance. This swing exchange took roughly two months.

Other leave strategies could be the point at which the value crosses beneath a moving normal (not appeared), or when a pointer, for example, the stochastic oscillator, crosses its signature line.

Exchange forex and CFDs on stock files, products, stocks, metals and energies with an authorized and controlled representative. For all customers who open their first genuine record, XM offers up to $5000 store reward to test the XM items and administrations with no underlying store required. Study how you can exchange more than 1000 instruments on the XM MT4 and MT5 stages from your PC and Mac, or an assortment of cell phones.

The amount Money Do I Need to Swing Trade Stocks?

Keen on swing exchanging stocks–taking exchanges that last a couple of days to half a month and thinking about what amount of cash you have to begin? How much capital you'll need is reliant on the procedure you use, which at that point influences the amount you chance per exchange and your position size. This article gives different situations to how a lot of money you'll have to swing exchange stocks a hazard controlled way, which will improve your opportunity of accomplishment.

Markets You Can Swing Trade

Swing exchanging is taking a place that could takethe most recent days to half a month (possibly several months for certain brokers/exchanges). To what extent a swing exchange keeps going relies upon the procedure you're utilizing and what you anticipate from your exchanges. If a stock normally moves 1% every day, and it needs to move 10% to arrive at your objective (where you need to get out with a benefit), it could take half a month or more before the value advances toward your leave point (if current conditions proceed).

Swing brokers hold positions medium-term, in contrast to informal investors (perceive How Much Money Do I Need to Become a Day Trader?) who close all situations before the day closes. Procedures shift by swing dealer; however, the first spotlight is on force swing traders need to catch a conventional piece of value development in the most limited measure of time conceivable. At the point when the value energy closes, swing brokers proceed onward to different chances.

This style of exchanging should be possible in many markets (stocks, forex, fates, and choices, for instance), which have the development you can benefit from (profit!). Swing exchanging stocks is well known because there's constantly a stock moving with force someplace

Forex is likewise mainstream because, for the most part, there's a money pair (or a few) that is moving admirably. Prospects are likewise exceptionally mainstream among day and swing traders, offering a wide cluster of items (for example, gold, bonds, stock records, instability, espresso, and so forth) to exchange. Swing exchanging forex requires less capital than stocks and fates and is hence a decent choice if you need more cash-flow to swing exchange stocks.

Looking at certain situations in the financial exchange, so you can perceive how a lot of cash you'll have to turn into a securities exchange swing trader.

Issue of Under-Capitalization When Swing Trading Stocks

Having more capital in your record is superior to less. One major slip-up dealers make being under-promoted. In the stock, advertise being under-promoted can without much of a stretch occur... particularly to new brokers if their record drops in worth.

As showed, to make it worth our time and energy, we ought to change in any event $100 per exchange. Along these lines, our victors won't be fundamentally disintegrated by commissions and expenses. However,if we hazard $100, what occurs if a dealer's record parity drops to $4,000? Presently they are gambling 2.5% on each exchange. Ifall don't go well, and the parity drops to $3,000, the broker is currently gambling 3.3% per exchange... they are gambling more as their presentation deteriorates!

If your record parity dips under $5,000, STOP TRADING, since you can never again bear to lose $100 and still keep the record hazard to under 2%. Likewise, if you opened a record with $15,000 and you said you would just hazard 1% exchange, if your parity falls beneath $10,000, quit exchanging. If you continue exchanging with an equalization beneath $10,000, you will hazard over 1% (gambling at any rate $100 per exchange).

Top up your record to bring it back above $5,000 (or $10,000 if gambling 1%) if you are as yet certain about your technique (or are eager to place in an opportunity to make it work), or just pick not to exchange until you are in a superior situation to do as such.

Cash Needed to Swing Trade Stocks – Final Word

The snappiest method to perceive how a lot of capital you need is to utilize the pursued equation:

exchange chance x position size x (100%/account hazard %) = Capital Required.

Expect your chance 1% of your record, purchase 100 offers, and your exchange hazard is $2 (purchase at $38 and stop misfortune at $36). Module the numbers:

$2 x 100 x 100 = $20,000. That is the amount you have to make that exchange. You could use influence (up to 2:1), which implies that you need $10K in the record to make this exchange because with influence, you will have the required $20K. You will need to have more in the record than the definite sum you need!

In case you're willing to change 2% of your record per exchange:

Record hazards and exchange hazards help you decide how much capital you will require. Each exchange is somewhat unique, with various exchange dangers and position sizes. Record for that when deciding the amount you will store. Concentrate the stock graphs, choose how and where you will enter and where you will put a stop misfortune.

When in doubt, you will require at any rate $5,000 to $10,000 to swing exchange stocks successfully. It is prescribed you store more than the base, supposing that you store the absolute minimum a couple losing exchanges will put you beneath the suggest record balance.

It's smarter to hold up a couple of months and set aside more capital than to surge in under-promoted and likely lose everything. Utilize an opportunity to rehearse while you set aside!

Swing Trading - How to Trade?

Fundamental learning:

It sounds incredible when you consider swing stock exchange; however, the majority of the brokers are unconscious of the technique on the best way to exchange in swing, exchanging the trader by and large revels into buying the stocks toward the path where the pattern is solid. In straightforward words, the swing trader will never exchange the course, which isn't in the stream and not coordinating up the pattern. These exchanges are hung on for a couple of days, and as a rule, they monitor the higher time allotment outlines, which is around 1 hour and more than that while you are observing and setting your exchanges.

There are a few recognized manners by which a swing dealer can without much of a stretch spot his/her exchanges and that additionally toward the prevalent pattern. The normal and helpful practice is to sit tight at the cost level to remake previously, and you have to enter your exchange before it reaches out towards on stream. The passage is done for the most part based on value resounding off of help or opposition levels, pattern lines, or by and large it might require marker check.

In swing stock exchanging, the swing financial specialists or brokers can without much of a stretch have the chances heaped in their benefit by watching the more prominent and greater time graphs and by entering the exchanges just the method for significant patterns in the securities exchange. It will make your business an incredible style of exchanging regardless of the securities exchange.

Figure out How to Swing Trade: In request to figure out how to swing exchange, you have to have the authority over the central segments of the exchanging. Every one of the subtleties that are talked about underneath structures the structure hinders the swing stock exchanging and are the reasons why outrageous expert financial specialists are extremely beneficial.

This territory grasps the accompanying:

o Trading brain science -

You have to create adjusted Psychology to wind up fit for exchanging effectively.

o The money the executives -

This administration allows a trader to limit the dangers and to expand the arrival esteem on their rewards.

o Market investigation -

To do the market assessment, two different ways are Technical and essential investigation.

o Japanese candle graphs -

It is the main component to have an inside investigationof the financial exchange and its feelings. You should be equipped to peruse and understand the Japanese candle arrangements.

o Trend Identification -

The swing brokers increment their chances by exchanging the course of the pattern. You have to discover the right pattern.

o Support and opposition levels -

These two levels grant the trader to locate the pivotal degrees of the securities exchange where the patterns are in the dealer's support.

o Fibonacci retracement levels -

Much the same as the help and obstruction levels, the Fibonacci retracement levels additionally enable you to have a decent passage into the market.

o Trading markers -

The apprentices must take a gander at the pointers, which are commonly utilized by the banks and expert financial specialists in swing exchanging.

o Stop misfortune -

Stop misfortunes bring about only a little harm; accordingly, it is disregarded by the majority of the newcomers around here.

o Trading hours -

Continuously cause a decent search, and after that, to find your hours that are appropriate for the opening and shutting of the trades...

Swing Trading: Swing Trading Stock That Help You Earn More

The term alludes to the different styles of swing exchanging stock, items, or list. This exchanging is a sort of exchanging practice where the trader purchases or sells the instrument at or close to the finish of a dor up value swing in the ware. This swing is caused either because of the day by day value unpredictability or week by week value instability. Information on these styles encourages him to become a beneficial dealer and puts him on the way of effective exchanging calling.

The time furthest reaches that is typically associated with holding the instrument by the trader is 1-4 days. It is, for the most part, not exactly seven days, regardless. The money or the swing is exchanging stock, which the trader is managing in swings starting with one value level then onto the next. A swing broker rides on this wavering or swing that the market makes on the stock. That implies he purchases the instruments toward market patterns, and he doesn't exchange by conflicting with the significant patterns in the market.

There are various manners by which he can put an exchange. The most well-known method for doing it toward market pattern is to sit tight at the costs swing, exchanging stock to return or backtrack and afterwards enter an exchange before it goes onwards. This is the most secure technique as he can stack the chances in support of him by watching the higher period graphs, and after that enters the exchange, the bearing of significant pattern likewise got back to the draw time. There are some essential components of swing exchanging that should be aced to turn into an effective dealer.

The above all else component in learning the swing exchanging business is a comprehension of the exchanging brain research. The other significant viewpoint requires knowledge of the significant patterns of the market. This causes him to distinguish the pattern effectively in the market and increase from it. The third significant viewpoint is the dealer's capacity to oversee cash with the goal that he can expand gains and limit dangers. The dealer ought to likewise have the option to peruse and comprehend the Japanese Candlestick development to get a vibe of the market opinions. Another component that is urgent to his prosperity is to have the option to discover the best exchanging hours to open and close the exchange.

Different fundamentals of a decent trader are to find what pointers are utilized by other expert dealers to run swing exchanging effectively. He should likewise be knowledgeable about the Trading markers utilized by different banks. He ought to have the option to distinguish the specialized market investigation and the essential market examination as the two most significant styles to break the market. Among other components of the swing exchanging business is the information of help and obstruction levels, Fibonacci retracement level, stop misfortune, and recognizable proof of pattern lines.

The dealer needs to acclimate himself with this data to begin his voyage to turning into an effective swing broker.

Swing Trading Stocks - An Insight to Pros and Cons

There are sure contrasts between Swing Trading Stocks and Day Trading. Day Trading is identified with a specific timeframe, though Swing exchanging likewise delineates a specific timeframe. Swing exchanging includes a timespan that is longer than the staring off into space-time range and shorter than somebody who is headed to contribute and exchange for a more extended timeframe. If there should be an occurrence of records and assessment purposes, whatever is not exactly a year is imagined as a transient exchanging the financial exchange, and anything that is about multi-year or more is considered as long haul evaluating.

Swing exchanging is a novel style of exchanging and venture. It is reasonable for each one of the individuals who need to exchange for a more extended timeframe than a day exchanging and have a decent learning of swing exchanging procedures. The informal investors enter and exit around the same time and in a similar position. The swing traders would leave their exchange of stocks and items to be open for a couple of weeks, which can stretch out as long as a couple of months. The traders work as indicated by the swing exchanging methodologies they know.

Swing Trading Stocks Pros and Cons:

Like all other things,Swing exchanging additionally has its high side and awful side. Bothe the day exchanging and swing trading are similarly dangerous, which relies upon the experience, specialized assessment, and brain science as upheld by the trader. Continuously recollect the standard that is, the more drawn out the time of exchange the market, the higher the hazard factor.

The Pros of Swing Trading Stocks-

*It is less tedious than the day exchanging segment.

*A dealer possesses more energy for the assessment of the best-exchanging methods between the exchanges, and like this, the broker can most likely choose great and fascinating entertainers.

*The first section, which is poor, is offered time to get recuperated from the harm and afterward go to a positive level or state-contingent upon the bearing the trader has chosen. It is prescribed that a long position that is upward positions are substantially more superior to the principal short position that is descending position.

*Swing Traders doesn't require to address the issues of the 'Example Day Trader.'

*Swing traders are permitted to have more information for concentrate as indicated by the time than the informal investors.

*A swing broker is progressively sure and certain about his/her exchange because the ongoing pattern of exchanging is bolstered by the long haul information from the history.

The Cons of Swing Trading Stocks-

*Definitely the swing trader consumes less time and possesses more energy for the assessment of the best-exchanging methods between the exchanges and accordingly, the dealer can likely choose great and fascinating entertainers.

The con: is that a swing trader may get awful information and subtleties into the information assessment and might choose a less valuable stock execution or lost stock or item.

*The first passage which is poor is offered time to get recuperated from the harm and after that go to a positive level or state-contingent upon the heading, the broker has chosen. It is suggested that a long position that is upward positions are substantially more superior to the primary short position that is descending position.

The Con: the main poor and awful section has the opportunity to get going the other way to the trade.....

HOW IT DIFFERS FROM OTHER TYPES OF TRADING AND WHERE IT IS APPLIED

Day Trading versus Swing Trading: What's the Difference?

Day Trading versus Swing Trading: An Overview

Dynamic traders frequently bunch themselves into two camps: the informal investors and the swing brokers. Both look to benefit from transient stock developments (versus long haul ventures), however, which exchanging technique is the better one? Here are the upsides and downsides of day exchanging as opposed to swinging exchanging, and the significant contrasts between the two.

Day exchanging, as the name proposes, includes making many exchanges a single day, because of specialized examination and modern outlining frameworks. The informal investor's goal is to bring home the bacon from exchanging stocks, products, or monetary forms, by making little benefits on various exchanges and topping misfortunes on unrewarding exchanges. Informal investors regularly don't keep any positions or possess any protections medium-term.

Day exchanging includes an extremely one of a kind range of abilities that can be hard to ace. Investopedia's Become a Day Trader course gives a top to bottom review of day exchanging, total with over five hours of on-request video. During the course, you will take in everything from request types to specialized examination strategies to augment your stable hazard returns.

Day Trading

The best snare of day trading is the potential for fabulous advantages. Nonetheless, this may simply be a probability for the unprecedented individual who has all of the properties, for instance, consummation, control, and consistency, required to transform into a productive casual financial specialist.

The U.S. Insurances and Exchange Commission (SEC) points out that "days facilitates consistently bear budgetary hardships in their first long times of trading, and various never graduate to profit-making status." While the SEC alarms that casual speculators should simply danger money they can remain to lose, various casual financial specialists cause huge disasters on got monies, either through margined trades or capital gained from family or various sources. These disasters may decrease their day trading calling just as put them in free commitment.

The casual financial specialist works alone, liberated from the driving forces of corporate big shots. He can have a versatile working schedule, get some truly necessary rest at whatever point required, and work at his pace, rather than someone on the corporate treadmill.

Casual financial specialists need to fight with high-repeat agents, theoretical stock investments, and other market specialists who consume millions to get trading focal points. In this condition, a casual financial specialist has an insignificant choice yet to burn through strongly on a trading stage, charting programming, front line PCs, etc. Advancing costs join costs for getting live worth articulations and commission costs that can incorporate due to the volume of trades.

Long-enduring casual financial specialists love the surge of setting their minds against the market and various specialists throughout the day consistently. The adrenaline flood from snappy fire trading is something generally scarcely any sellers will admit to, yet it is a central point in their decision to make a few bucks from trading. It's sketchy such people would be substance experiencing their days selling devices or poring over numbers in an office workspace.

To genuinely make a go at it, a seller must stop his everyday business and give up his suffering normally planned check. Starting there on, the casual financial specialist must depend through and through without any other individual skill and attempts to deliver enough advantage to deal with the tabs and welcome a not all that terrible lifestyle.

Day trading is upsetting because of the need to watch different screens to spot trading openings, and from that point onward, the exhibit quickly to abuse them. This must be accomplished for a long time, and the essential for such a significant level of focus and focus can consistently provoke burnout.

For some employments in money, having the correct degree from the right college is essential only for a meeting. Day exchanging, interestingly, doesn't require costly instruction from an Ivy League school. While there are no formal instructive necessities for turning into an informal investor, courses in the specialized investigation and mechanized exchange might be useful.

Swing Trading

Swing exchanging depends on distinguishing swings in stocks, wares, and monetary forms that occur over a time of days. A swing exchange may take a couple of days to half a month to work out. In contrast to an informal investor, a swing dealer isn't probably going to make exchanging a full-time vocation.

Anybody with information and speculation capital can have a go at swing exchanging. The drawn-out time period (from days to weeks instead of minutes to hours), a swing trader shouldn't be stuck to his PC screen throughout the day. He can even keep up a different all-day work (as long as he isn't checking to exchange screens all the time at work).

Exchanges, for the most part, need time to work out. Keeping an exchange for an advantage open for a couple of days or weeks may bring about higher benefits than exchanging and out of similar security on numerous occasions a day.

Since swing exchanging, as a rule, includes positions held in any event medium-term, edge necessities are higher. Most extreme influence is typically multiple times one's capital. Contrast this and day exchanging where edges are multiple times one's capital.

The swing dealer can set stop misfortunes. While there is a danger of a quit being executed at a troublesome value, it beats the regular observing of every single vacant position that is an element of day exchanging.

Likewise, with any style of exchanging, swing exchanging can bring about significant misfortunes. Since swing dealers hold their situations for longer than informal investors, they likewise risk bigger misfortunes.

Since swing exchanging is rarely an all-day work, there is considerably less shot of burnout because of stress. Swing dealers, as a rule, have a customary activity or another wellspring of pay from which they can counterbalance or relieve exchanging misfortunes.

Swing exchanging should be possible with only one PC and traditional exchanging devices. It doesn't require the best in class innovation of day exchanging.

Key Differences

Day exchanging and swing exchanging each has points of interest and disadvantages. Neither one of the strategies is superior to the next, and brokers ought to pick the methodology that works best for their aptitudes, inclinations, and way of life. Day exchanging is more qualified for people who are energetic about exchanging full time and have the three Ds: definitiveness, control, and industriousness (essentials for fruitful day exchanging).

Day exchanging achievement likewise requires a propelled comprehension of specialized exchanging and outlining. Since day exchanging is serious and distressing, traders ought to have the option to remain quiet and control their feelings enduring an onslaught. At last, day exchanging includes hazard—traders ought to be set up to now and again leave with 100 percent misfortunes.

Swing exchanging, then again, doesn't require such a considerable arrangement of attributes. Since swing exchanging can be embraced by anybody with some venture capital and doesn't require full-time consideration, it is a feasible alternative for brokers who need to keep there all day employments, yet besides, fiddle with the business sectors. Swing brokers ought to likewise have the option to apply a mix of essential and specialized investigation, as opposed to specialized examination alone.

Nugget

Day exchanging, as the name recommends, includes making many exchanges a single day, in light of specialized examination and modern outlining frameworks.

Swing exchanging depends on recognizing swings in stocks, wares, and monetary forms that happen over a time of days.

Neither one of the strategies is superior to the next, and traders ought to pick the methodology that works best for their abilities, inclinations, and way of life.

More on day trading and swing trading

Day exchanging and swing exchanges share two things. The two styles of exchanging would like to profit from short moves in the market. They are not for the swoon of heart. To counterbalance the hazard, there is additionally the probability of extraordinary returns! There is nothing that looks at the enthusiasm of finishing an exceptionally effective exchange. A portion of these exchanges will take a minute ago and some up to a few days. By and by, I appreciate day exchanging, and swing exchanges are utilized less yet at the same time, hold extraordinary benefit potential.

Day exchanging and swing exchanges are distinctive in that swing exchanges are less adaptable. Day exchanging defenders get out toward the finish of consistently however are regularly doing various exchanges every day. One of the qualities of this is knowing where you remain at the end of every day. Swing exchanges may complete in a day or more, yet are similarly prone to keep going for a couple of days, and throughout an exchange, there are bound to be more good and bad times in productivity. There is potential to procure more from each swing exchange. However, there are dangers. Day exchanging and swing exchanging likely could be your pass to stopping the everyday employment if you so want.

Day exchanging has no medium-term dangers, as long as all exchanges are shut before the market close, swing exchanges are increasingly defenseless to news or financial atmosphere during the exchanging day or around evening time. This news can harm your situation, outside the ability to control the swing exchange framework. Day exchanging or swing exchanging without a framework will undoubtedly be unbeneficial.

Day exchanging or swing exchanging frameworks start at $2000 and go up from that point. Many methodologiesof various brokers take to build up a triumphant framework. How you make your framework for exchanging can be a good blend of ways of thinking, yet the most significant thing is to adhere to your framework. The up Or market bearing does not affect. There are, in every case, huge open doors in day exchanging and swing exchanges an assortment of business sectors.

It is conceivable to exchange a couple of stocks all the time, as long as they adhere to your foreordained arrangement of standards for exchange signals. Exchanging a similar round of stocks has the additional impetus that you start to discover what a stock is probably going to do when diverse news or monetary components happen. If you have a solid stock pick asset, to begin with, it encourages you to screen out the terrible and discover new stocks.

Scalping versus Swing Trading: The Difference To Spot

Scalping versus Swing Trading: An Overview

Many take an interest in the securities exchanges, some as financial specialists, others as dealers. Contributing is executed considering a long haul see—years or even decades. Exchanging, in the meantime, moves to pocket gains all the time.

A typical strategy for recognizing one sort of dealer from another is the timeframe for which a broker holds a stock—a change that can extend from a couple of moments to months or even years.

The most prominent exchanging systems incorporate day exchanging, swing exchanging, scalping, and position exchanging. Picking a style which suits your very exchanging personality is fundamental for long haul achievement. This article spreads out the contrasts between a scalping procedure and a swing exchanging system.

Nugget

Scalping and swing exchanging are two of the more famous transient contributing systems utilized by dealers.

Scalping includes making several exchanges day by day, which positions are held quickly, now and then only seconds; all things considered, benefits are little. However, the hazard is additionally diminished.

Swing exchanging utilizes specialized examination and diagrams to pursue and benefit off patterns in stocks; the time span is middle of the road term, regularly a couple of days to half a month.

Scalping Methodology

Scalping methodology targets minor changes in intra-day stock value development, now and again entering and leaving all through the exchanging session, to manufacture benefits.

Regularly named a subtype of the day exchanging strategy, scalping includes various exchanges of exceptionally short holding periods from a couple of moments to minutes. Since positions are held for such brief periods, gains on a specific exchange (or benefits per exchange) are little; thus, scalpers do various exchanges—into the hundreds during a normal exchanging day—to assemble benefit. Constrained time presentation to the market lessens scalper chance.

Scalpers are fast, only from time to time, embracing a specific example. Scalpers go short in one exchange, at that point long in the following, little open doors are their objectives. Ordinarily working around the offer ask spread—purchasing on the offer and selling at ask—scalpers misuse the spread for benefit. Such changes to effectively adventure are more typical than huge moves, as even genuinely still markets minor observer developments.

Scalpers more often than not pursue brief period graphs, for example, 1-minute outlines, 5-minute diagrams, or exchange based tick graphs, to study value development of and accept approaches certain exchanges.

Scalpers look for sufficient liquidity for its similarity with the recurrence of exchanging. Access to precise information (quote framework, live feed) just as the capacity to quickly execute exchanges is a need for these traders. High commissions will, in general, lessen benefit with successive purchasing and selling, as they increment expenses of performing exchanges, so immediate agent access is commonly liked.

Scalping is most appropriate for the individuals who can commit time to the business sectors, remain focused, and act quickly. It's generally said that anxious individuals make great scalpers as they will, in general, exit from an exchange when it winds up beneficial. Scalping is for the individuals who can deal with pressure, settle on snappy choices, and act in like manner.

Your time period impacts what exchanging style is best for you; scalpers make many exchanges every day and must remain stuck to the business sectors, while swing dealers make fewer exchanges and can check in less as often as possible.

The methodology of swing exchanging includes distinguishing the pattern, at that point playing inside it. For instance, swing brokers would more often than not pick an emphatically inclining stock after a redress or combination, and just before it's prepared to rise once more, they would exit after taking some benefit. Such purchasing and selling techniques are rehashed to harvest gains.

In cases wherein stocks fall through help, traders move to the opposite side, going short. Ordinarily, swing traders are "pattern supporters," if there is an upswing, they go long, and if the general pattern is towards the drawback, they could go short. Swing exchanges stay open from a couple of days to half a month (near term)— in some cases even to months (transitional term), however, regularly enduring just a couple of days. Regarding time period, persistence required, and potential returns, swing exchanging falls between day exchanging and pattern exchanging. Swing dealers utilize specialized examination and graphs which show value activities, helping them find the best purposes of passage and exit for productive exchanges. These traders study obstruction and backing, utilizing Fibonacci expansions incidentally joined with different examples and specialized pointers. Some unpredictability is solid for swing exchanging as it offers to ascend to circumstances. Swing traders keep up cautiousness for a capability of more noticeable gains by enjoying fewer stocks, keeping business expenses low. The methodology functions admirably for those incapable of remaining stuck fulltime to the business sectors, keeping a moment by moment track of things. Low maintenance brokers who set aside an effort to look at what's going on during work interims regularly decide on this system. Pre-market and post-advertise audits are vital to fruitful swing exchanging, as is tolerance with medium-term possessions. Hence, it's not for the individuals who get on edge in such circumstances.

CPSIA information can be obtained
at www.ICGtesting.com
Printed in the USA
BVHW090821070521
606415BV00005BA/1555